The Manager's Guide to Conducting Interviews

On the other side of the table – plan and execute excellent
interviews to get the right person for the job

Stephen W. Walker

Impackt Publishing
We Mean Business

The Manager's Guide to Conducting Interviews

First published: September 2014

Production reference: 1240914

Published by Impackt Publishing Ltd.
Livery Place
35 Livery Street
Birmingham B3 2PB, UK.

ISBN 978-1-78300-012-8

www.Impacktpub.com

Credits

Author

Stephen W. Walker

Reviewers

Dr. Margaret Stockham Turner

José Urdaneta

Robert D. Watkins

Commissioning Editor

Richard Gall

Copy Editors

Tanvi Bhatt

Paul Hindle

Project Coordinator

Venitha Cutinho

Proofreaders

Simran Bhogal

Ameesha Green

Paul Hindle

Graphics

Sheetal Aute

Production Coordinator

Melwyn D'sa

Cover Work

Simon Cardew

About the Author

Stephen W. Walker has published numerous articles and speaks at various conferences. He has over 30 years of management experience in globally competitive sectors. He has interviewed and recruited dozens of people and shares his experience on how to choose the best candidate in this book.

He co-founded Motivation Matters in 2004, which is a vehicle to deliver greater organizational performance, with his managerial behavior consultancy. He has worked for notable organizations such as Corning, De La Rue, and Buhler, and has been hired to help Philips, Lloyds TSB, and many others.

His expertise is the managerial behavior that drives good team performance. Competent interviewing is a fundamental skill in the effective manager's portfolio of skills. Further information about him is available at www.motivationmatters.co.uk.

A book is a significant piece of work, and I wrote this over 8 months. I wish to acknowledge the more, and less, subtle shepherding of the Impackt editors to bring the book to this point. Their combination of editorial acuity and patience was marked. In particular, Richard Gall pointed out improvements to the words and structure that significantly improved the book.

The book's reviewers, Dr. Margaret Stockham and Mr. Anton Ratnayake, deserve my gratitude for accepting the task on top of their already busy lives. Their comments improved the readability and value of the book.

I am also grateful for the support of my family and friends who suffered every missed deadline, every anxious day of writer's block, and every frustrated rewrite with a wry smile and warm heart. First amongst those is my wife, Anne, who's professional proofreading skills have been put to maximum use to marshal the thoughts into the coherent body of work that now exists. Finally, I dedicate this book to my son, Sam, who is just taking his first step on the management ladder. I hope this book helps you, and everyone starting out on their management career, to achieve the success you deserve. Thank you all.

About the Reviewers

Dr. Margaret Stockham Turner trained as a chartered physiotherapist before developing a career in healthcare management. She has 20 years of board-level experience in healthcare in the UK, Sweden, and the USA, including three times as NHS Chief Executive.

As the founder of Partners in Practice Ltd., she is now a highly effective and sought after management consultant who regularly provides advisory services and development support to the Department of Health, national bodies, pharmaceutical and healthcare technology industries, and Clinical Commissioners.

Margaret is also the Non-exec Chair of an innovative international biotech company and a trustee on the board of a local mental health charity. She has published numerous professional articles and modules for the Open University.

José Urdaneta is a multi-certified project manager and IT specialist. For 17 years, he has been responsible for the system architecture, design, specification, project management, and structured execution of complex IT systems, defining the essential core design features and elements that provide the framework for multi-tier, cross-platform systems. He works in all areas of SDLC and ALM as a system integrator, providing oversight and direction in all aspects of architecture, software development, and product and service delivery, including achievement of quality-level activities in support of business goals.

He leads both small, agile teams with 5-10 people to big teams with 10-30 people. He has vast experience in enterprise architecture, systems design, program management, and full accountability for profit\loss. He executes multi-million dollar programs, manages IT services, and directs the product deployment to market on complex applications.

He is Director of Systems Assurance, Testing, and IT at DRC. He has a background in engineering and IT, and he has over 17 years of expertise in program management of complex IT system developments. He is the Chief Systems Architect in all the phases of software development at TeleworX. He is responsible for Configuration Management (CM) and Quality Assurance (QA) and Testing in TeleworX's agile XP programming cycles using Visual Studio Team System (2010). He brings his previous experience as a certified CMMI Assessor and SCAMPI practitioner and applies his rich experience in consulting and IT management across every phase of the SDLC.

He leads a diverse team of testers and is responsible for the development, planning, execution, tracking, and reporting of Testing Metrics, up to and including areas of regression, functional, stress, and load testing.

Prior to joining TeleworX in 2005, he enjoyed 10 years of a successful engineering, IT, and management career with Science Applications International Corporation (SAIC) as a Senior Systems Analyst. While at SAIC, he acted as Project Manager in many IT initiatives for both government and commercial clients. He also managed concurrent large-scale IT projects and participated as a manager of various Independent Verification and Validation (IV&V) initiatives in projects running at CMMI Level 3. He began his early career in the IT field first as a programmer for safety review systems for Processing Plants and quickly evolved as an experienced IT Technical Program Manager.

His directive for process improvements means he is involved in systems architecture, where he coordinates all system Operational and Acceptance testing activities; test planning, execution, and communication, where he facilitates production readiness decisions and obtains final approval before scheduling implementation; and Quality Assurance/Process Improvement, where he provides leadership to support staff to establish the test knowledge base, and establish and maintain a common test repository.

He holds an MBA degree, obtained with honors, in Management of Information Systems from George Washington University, DC, a Masters in Science degree in Environmental Engineering from Columbia University, NY, and a BS degree in Chemical Engineering from Metropolitan University, Venezuela. He holds Master Project Management credentials from ANSI, ITIL V3 certification. He is a Certified Scrum Master, holds Six Sigma certification, and holds an accreditation of Certified Software Tester (CSTE) from the Quality Assurance Institute (QAI).

His LinkedIn profile can be found at http://www.linkedin.com/pub/jose-urdaneta-csm-itil-v3/22/683/496/.

His professional web page can be found at http://joseurdaneta.weebly.com/.

Robert D. Watkins has been in the information technology industry since 1995 as a contractor and consultant to several Fortune 500 firms. From the outset, he has parlayed his passion for learning new skills, new technologies, and methodologies, resulting in his achievement of Microsoft and Cisco certifications.

The second phase of his career began in 1999 with a dual role as both a Y2K implementation project manager and systems engineer for an insurance office located in Pittsburgh, PA. Finding project consulting his niche, he continued pursuing subsequent clients in the Petroleum, Publishing, and Consumer Products industries. Over the next 8 years, he planned and executed more than 100 projects related to IT and process improvement.

In 2007, he began the third phase of his career by taking a 2 year sabbatical from consulting to complete his Business Administration degree. His degree was completed in parallel with strategic planning and project activities with several entrepreneurial start-ups as a management consultant. Since achieving his BSBA degree in 2009, Robert has been engaged as a Senior Project Manager, Management Consultant, and Acting CIO/COO for several start-ups. He continues to pursue entrepreneurial engagements and projects, including the occasional consulting editor role in the new digital publishing industry.

He has been a contributing author in the following technical certification guides:

> ➤ MCSE Migrating from Windows NT to Windows 2000 Study Guide
> (Exam 70-222 - ISBN-13: 978-0072127119)

> ➤ CCNA Test Yourself Practice Exams, 2nd Edition
> (Exam 640-507 - ISBN-13: 978-0072126686)

He is the consulting editor on the first in a series of Little Paper Umbrellas - a Zoe Bird Mystery, 1st Edition (ASIN: B00EIMMMIY | ISBN-13: 978-1492943372 / ISBN-10: 1492943371)

A special thanks to my wife Vicky for her patience and support through all the phases of my career and my life; I couldn't have done it without her.

Contents

Preface

There is a commonly used phrase in recruitment: "Hire for attitude, train for skills."

The meaning is simply that you can give someone new skills more easily than you can change their innate attitude. There is, though, a common sense balance to be achieved; a minimum level of skill is necessary. You wouldn't want to hire an airline pilot on the basis of positive attitude alone! Depending on the job, and the mix of skills in the team, you have a choice about the skill level you could hire.

Assessing someone's attitude is not that easy though. Attitude is internal to a person and can only be assessed through behavior. In an interview, you are assessing the candidate through responses to your questions. This book will teach you how to understand those questions, how to assess the responses, and how to ask follow up questions to give you the evidence you need to make a judgment.

By the end of this book, you will be fully conversant with interview techniques, you will have practiced your interview presentations, and you will be able to score the candidate's responses to drive the selection process. You will also understand how to reach a consensus after the interview, discussing your thoughts and refining the pool of candidates to ensure that you get the right person for the job.

What this book covers

Chapter 1, Before the Interview – Preparing and Practicing, will take you through the preliminary stages of the interview process, ranging from gathering information about the candidates to building up your own confidence to ensure you run the interview effectively and professionally.

Chapter 2, Starting the Interview – Greeting and Settling, will guide you in effectively and confidently managing the early stages of the interview, setting the tone for the interview.

Chapter 3, Conducting the Interview – Questioning and Scoring, will give you information and practical guidance on how to assess the candidates with effective questions and how to score them.

Chapter 4, After the Interview – Agreeing and Deciding, will help you to organize your thoughts following the interview by reviewing your scoring and working through any doubts or concerns you may have to reach a final decision.

Who this book is for

This book has been written to give managers looking to interview and hire a new team member a step-by-step guide that leads to a successful recruitment.

The book is focused on the needs of a manager, whether they are new to management and have never interviewed before or they just want to find a reliable companion to help them to sharpen their skills and build their confidence.

Recruiting your first person for your team is a very important task. A manager is responsible for the performance of their team. Who you choose to be on that team says a lot about you. You also need to make a good choice so that you, and your team, perform well.

Conventions

In this book, you will find a number of styles of text that distinguish between different kinds of information. Here are some examples of these styles, and an explanation of their meaning.

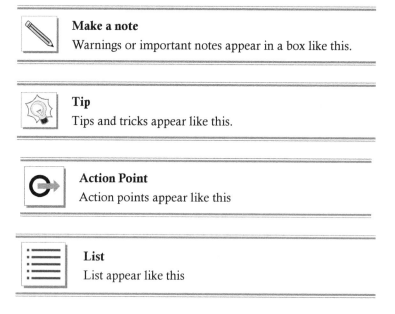

Make a note

Warnings or important notes appear in a box like this.

Tip

Tips and tricks appear like this.

Action Point

Action points appear like this

List

List appear like this

Reader feedback

Feedback from our readers is always welcome. Let us know what you think about this book—what you liked or may have disliked. Reader feedback is important for us to develop titles that you really get the most out of.

To send us general feedback, simply send an e-mail to feedback@impacktpub.com, and mention the book title via the subject of your message.

If there is a book that you need and would like to see us publish, please send us a note via the **Submit Idea** form on https://www.impacktpub.com/#!/bookidea.

Piracy

Piracy of copyright material on the Internet is an ongoing problem across all media. At Packt, we take the protection of our copyright and licenses very seriously. If you come across any illegal copies of our works, in any form, on the Internet, please provide us with the location address or website name immediately so that we can pursue a remedy.

Please contact us at copyright@impacktpub.com with a link to the suspected pirated material.

We appreciate your help in protecting our authors, and our ability to bring you valuable content.

>1

Before the Interview – Preparing and Practicing

In this chapter, I will teach you about the information gathering and confidence building tools you need to excel as an interviewer. You can prepare and practice these topics to perfection before you interview anyone. You will learn how to do the following:

> ➤ Determine the job specification
> ➤ Gather information from HR
> ➤ Manage the interview
> ➤ Keep the interview legal
> ➤ Prepare yourself for the interview
> ➤ Prepare the opening introductions
> ➤ Be your best in the interview—performance mode
> ➤ Prepare the candidate for interview

By the end of this chapter, you will have worked through the preparations you need to be confident and at ease when conducting an interview. Knowing what to do is not the same as being able to do it though! This chapter is the foundation for the interviewing skills we are developing in you. A solid foundation is essential before moving to the next stage. I want you to do the preparation, put in the work, and keep practicing until you are perfect in each of the fifteen topics in this chapter.

As a gray-haired ex-manager, I can tell you that my focus is always on performance, that of both myself and my team. A good interviewer will create a job opportunity that is a perfect match for the chosen candidate. I will try to pass on my experience of interviewing as clearly as possible, but most importantly, I want you to focus on your own performance as an interviewer. If you are focused and committed to improving and developing your skills, you will become a noticeably good interviewer—you will wow people with your interviewing skills!

If you're ready, let's make a start.

Determining the job specification

The first consideration is whether the job or jobs you are looking to fill are needed for:

> ➤ A new team duplicating an existing team

> ➤ An addition to an existing team

> ➤ A new function in an existing team

> ➤ A new team with a new function

> ➤ A demand fluctuation

A discussion with your manager is needed to find out what is required.

The simplest situation—duplicating an existing team—suggests the job and skills specifications, interview questions, and scoring methodology that **Human Resources** (**HR**) previously determined are still relevant and useable.

If you are looking to recruit an additional team member for a team that has an unchanged role to perform, you must be aware of the strengths and weaknesses of the team, including yourself. The people in the team, and those coming for interview, are not Lego bricks. When you try to assemble them into a working team, you will discover different skill sets, which means the new recruits have to fill in the weaknesses as well as offer the basic skills.

This will require the score sheet to be reviewed in light of the emphasized need for certain skills; those skills may need a higher weighting factor. You will learn about the score sheets in *Chapter 3, Conducting the Interview – Questioning and Scoring*.

Sometimes you may be looking to expand the capability of an existing team and are looking for new skills. This can come about through innovation in the team's processes, a future need, or your manager's experience of how the present team operates.

This new capability may need new skills, and the HR information will need to be modified to suit this new requirement. Apart from understanding the existing team, you will need to incorporate the new skills requirement into the interview documentation in cooperation with HR.

Finally, a new team with a new function will need all the job and skills specifications, interview questions, and scoring methodology to be created anew.

You may also be recruiting to cover demand fluctuations leading to lower-than-acceptable service levels. An understanding of the demand and team capacity fluctuations is essential to recruit to sustain team performance in those situations.

Whatever is the reason for the recruitment, you can explore the issues through a discussion with your manager and then ensure that HR amends the documentation as needed.

Gathering information from Human Resources

The first step is to collect the basic information about the position you are trying to fill from HR.

Interviews are stressful, not only for the candidate being interviewed, but for you as the interviewer as well! You want to be perfectly prepared for conducting the interview to avoid any embarrassing mistakes. Your performance as an interviewer is also key to putting the candidate at ease. A nervous candidate will not interview well. You don't want to worry that the basic information is wrong. As a manager, you will need to exude confidence to keep your staff content and working towards your objectives. That confidence comes from making sure you have as few surprises as possible, and that comes from careful and thorough preparation.

HR should provide you with the following documents:

> ➤ The functional, technical, and business specifications for the job
> ➤ The candidate pack
> ➤ The interview questions with follow up questions

Check that the job specification and the candidate pack are correct. The requirements may have changed since having a discussion with your manager, for instance, the skills required for the job that you're interviewing for may have been altered; this could also apply to the location, salary range, and so on. In some cases, HR may not have picked up on those changes. You don't want to find out that you and your HR representative are not on the same page about the job with respect to the questions in the interview! The entire interview process could be a waste of time if the information is wrong.

HR usually advertises or searches for candidates. Ask to look at the advert and/or candidate specification to check if it is suitable. Most often, HR will handle the queries and correspondence with candidates.

To choose who to interview, you need to have a clear specification of what the essential attributes of the job are. I suggest you set a specification that gives you a handful of interviews.

Your organization may also research the candidates' social media profiles. Facebook and LinkedIn are the more obvious channels to get a background picture of a candidate.

We will cover illegal discrimination later in this chapter, but the use of background information, unless agreed to or declared by the candidate, is fraught with difficulty as the law is still being established case by case. It would be sensible to have a permission checkbox on the application form to gain the candidate's permission to do the social media profiling.

Tip
Make a note of the decision making criteria used to select candidates for interview in case you have to show the decision was not founded on illegal discrimination.

When it is time to hold the interview, you will have the candidate's application form, curriculum vitae, letters, and e-mails to consider.

Check with HR what the arrangements are for the interviews. It is usually HR who collects the candidates from your reception, gives health and safety information, offers the usual facilities, and then show them out after the interview. You must make sure these arrangements have been made before the candidates arrive!

Next, we will find out how you can create an interview experience that reflects your values. This marks you out as different (in a good way!) and starts the process of building your managerial authority with the candidates and your organization.

Managing the interview

The interview has to be managed with respect to time, getting enough information from the candidate to make a decision, and to keep the interview on topic.

It is very easy to get sidetracked by an interesting candidate and run out of time.

This is one of the most difficult tasks for a new manager, so we are going to work through some techniques you need to prepare to help you manage the interview.

Specifically, we will learn how to do the following:

➤ Arrange the interview room

➤ Manage the sequence of questions

➤ Create a timetable and stick to it

It was once thought clever to arrange the interview room to place the candidate at a disadvantage. Later in this chapter, we will work through the need and means to relax the candidate to make them communicate freely. An interview is a discussion, not an interrogation.

I want you to make sure the interview room meets the following points:

➤ Do not seat the interviewers so the candidate has to look from side to side to see their faces. Keep the interview as conversational as possible.

➤ Seat the candidate within normal conversation distance.

➤ Try to avoid having a barrier between you. You may feel a desk is appropriate, but avoid things like open laptops and excessive amounts of paper.

➤ Don't seat the interview panel in front of a window so the candidate struggles to see the facial gestures.

➤ Seat everyone at the same height.

Interviews sometimes take place in small offices that are ill-equipped to seat everyone you have on your interviewing panel. If you need a bigger office to hold the interviews, go and get one.

Tip

You may have learnt by now that I want you to develop your own managerial style, your own personal brand. This is part of your development as a new manager. I want people to know what you stand for, what your values are, what makes you special.

This does not mean you can be a pain in the backside by insisting on something that doesn't matter. It means you will insist on things being done properly. By properly, I mean the way you want them done.

Next, you need to become familiar with the interview questions and how they are used to gather evidence to judge the candidate's match to the job requirements.

The interview structure

At this point, you should have already checked that the job and skillset specifications are correct. Also, you should have organized who will ask what, when, and how in the interview.

Now you need to understand how the interview questions should be asked to the candidate to describe his or her skills. The follow up questions are used to clarify the strength of those skills.

Tip

Two to four interviewers are typical for any job interview. Each interviewer asks a series of three to five questions, with follow up questions as needed.

Start with open ended questions and, if necessary, follow up with more closed questions to get a definite answer. For example, consider employing a structure similar to the following:

➤ Tell me about a time when you (for example) wrote creatively?

➤ Can you give me an example of the rules and guidance you had to follow?

➤ What did you do to adopt those rules and guidance?

You can dig down and judge the candidate's degree of skill by their answers:

- ➤ HR will give you the questions and score sheet.
- ➤ Work through every question and its follow up to understand what is being asked. Think about what the best possible response to each question would be.
- ➤ Decide on the minimum level for each skill the job requires.

Remember, we talked about making the interview as near to a conversation as possible. Schedule sufficient time for the level of detail you want; nothing destroys the rapport and communication in an interview as quickly as running out of time.

Managing the timetable

As a new manager, you may not have had many opportunities to plan yet. You should plan out the timetable of the interview.

A plan is not a set of definite instructions. It will say your introduction of the organization will last for around two minutes (or whatever), not that you have to stop talking after two minutes. You can be quite sure of how long your presentations will take because you will have practiced it and measured the time required.

You can judge how long the questions will take and how many questions will be asked. You can't know how long the candidate's replies will be, but you can make a good estimation. It is a good idea to state the time you have allowed for the interview when explaining the interview process to the candidate.

You can measure the progress the interview is making and compare it to the planned times. You will have the chance to review your planned times after conducting a few interviews as you will have real data to modify your plan.

There should always be some slack time between interviews. The interviewers will need to use that time to do the following:

- ➤ Finish marking the score sheets and any notes (revisit the discrimination section in this chapter if you have forgotten the rules)
- ➤ Put away (out of the candidate's eyesight) the previous candidate's documentation
- ➤ Take a short comfort break and drink some water
- ➤ Refresh their minds about the next candidate by reading through the documentation

When you are planning your timetable, you should be aware that this slack time can be used as a buffer if the interview does overrun. It is very bad practice to make a candidate wait because you haven't planned the timetable properly! The candidate is not going to be impressed by your management, which is not a good start to a manager-subordinate relationship.

Most management training includes planning. As a new manager, you need to learn the difference between theory and practice. To help you cross that divide, we are going to use an interview planning template. I can't know what your precise interview needs are, so the template includes a lot of variables.

Remember to be as accurate as possible with regard to the known tasks, such as your introductions. Carefully estimate how long the other tasks need.

We'll work through the planning now as follows:

1. **Fetching the candidate and seating them in the interview room**: It is a good idea for you to go and time how long this takes. Record the time.

2. **Casual conversation to settle the candidate**: This casual conversation begins the process of your understanding of the candidate. The conversation should be about trivialities *not connected to the job*. You can ask about the candidate's journey but avoid any comment that suggests a difficult journey is a negative on the candidate's score. You can talk about a significant recent event: sport, weather, the Stock Exchange, celebrity gossip. Avoid any topic that relates to the job as you are not interviewing yet. There is a section on building rapport near the end of this chapter.

   I suggest a time between one and two minutes for this, depending on your organization's practice. The candidate settling time you need depends on the candidate's nervousness. You will need to be prepared to start the interview if the candidate seems unable to settle. Estimate your time for this settling and then refine it through experience.

3. **Introducing the interviewers**: Practice the introduction of the interviewers by saying out loud what you will say to the candidate. It is important to speak it and time it as we talk twice as fast in our heads. You might introduce the interview panel by giving each person's name and job function. For example—"Can I introduce Ms. Smith and Mr. Jones of HR and myself, John Brown, the manager of the position we are interviewing for today." Prepare and time your interviewer introductions. Record the time.

4. **Explain the interview process**: This is a pre-prepared speech, so you will know how long this takes to deliver. Record the time.

5. **Ask if the candidate has any questions about the interview process**: If you have done a good job of explaining the process, there should not be any questions. If candidates frequently ask similar questions, you should add the points to your speech. I suggest you allow 30 seconds for a candidate's questions until your interview experience brings better information. It is always a good idea to reflect on your interviews to make changes to improve the process. However, it is inadvisable to change the interview process in the middle of a cycle of interviews. You should always interview following one standard process to avoid accusations of discrimination. If you decide to improve the interview process, do it between cycles.

Some organizations video their interviews, but ensure the candidates are informed of this practice. Alternatively, you may include a note taker in addition to the interview panel. You will be surprised how difficult it is to recall details of a candidate's responses at the end of a long day's interviewing.

6. **Introducing the organization and the job**: This is a prepared speech, so you know exactly how long this will take. Record the time.

7. **Ask if the candidate has any questions about the job or the organization**: Once again, if you have done a thorough job of explaining everything, there should not be any questions. Rewrite your speech if the same questions come up over and over. You need to make an estimate for the question time; I propose you allow 45 seconds in total.

8. **Ask the interview questions**: We will learn more about questioning in *Chapter 3, Conducting the Interview – Questioning and Scoring*. You have a list of primary questions and follow up questions from HR. You have agreed who is asking what primary questions and in what sequence. In my experience, you do not need to ask the follow up questions in every case. You will find that the candidate will sometimes give a full answer that allows the interviewers to score that skill or experience. Unless it is organizational policy to ask all the questions of every candidate, which may stem from anti-discrimination legislation, I suggest you assume half the primary questions will need the follow up questions.

    As an example, say there are ten primary questions with two follow up questions each. You will ask ten primary and ten follow up questions. Say the questions out loud and time how long they take to ask. Record the time.

9. **Listen to the candidate's answers**: This is a major variable that you cannot directly control. As a new manager, you need to find out about the response variation between people, and this is a big one. A candidate may just give an answer straight out. Alternatively, the candidate may think for 30 seconds or more. You will have to make a judgment on whether the candidate is still nervous or is carefully assembling a story. The primary interview questions are designed to encourage the candidate to give a full answer. Your follow up questions may be designed for an open-ended response or a simple yes or no answer. If the candidate has not made clear their experience in Excel spreadsheet design for example, you can ask, "Have you ever designed a spreadsheet?" Most candidates will give both quick and slow answers. It is usual for some of the answers to be probed more deeply. For example, the candidate may answer with, "We completed the project successfully." You will want to probe what "we" means and what the candidate did on the project team. Estimate how long their answers will be by answering the questions yourself. For 20 percent of the questions, allow time to ask three follow up questions. Say the words and time how long they take. Record the time you estimate for all the candidate's answers.

10. **Closing the interview**: After the questions have been answered, it is polite to ask if the candidate has any questions. Estimate a time for this and sharpen the estimate through experience; I suggest you begin with three minutes.

11. **Escorting the candidate**: After the interview is finished, the candidate needs to be escorted to reception or HR, or whatever your practice may be. Your time is precious at this critical stage, so please try and get someone else, not an interviewer, to take the candidate away. It will take time for the candidate to be taken away. Estimate the time and record it.

12. **Complete the score sheets and finish thinking**: You need time to think about what you have just heard and to come to your conclusion on the scoring and any issues that still concern you. I will deal with scoring in the next chapter, but it is important that you are settled with your scoring before moving to the next candidate. As an inexperienced manager, you will be astonished how after a full day of interviews you can remember so little about individual candidates! When you are interviewing, you have all your senses on high alert and your mind racing to understand what is said, assess the candidate, and manage the timetable. It is an extremely exhausting task. If it isn't exhausting, you haven't been sufficiently engaged in the interview! As well as time to complete the scoring, you need time for a comfort break. I suggest you allow ten to fifteen minutes in total for this. You can always revise your timetable in light of your own experience.

13. **Make a timetable**: Take the times you have recorded and make a timetable showing how many minutes each activity in the interview process should last.

You can then put in a few milestones to allow you to manage the interview. As an example, if the interview starts at 10am and the candidate settling and introductory speeches are estimated at fifteen minutes, then you have a milestone at 10.15am of when you should be starting to ask the interview questions.

Don't have too many or too few milestones. Spread them throughout the interview to give regular feedback of how the interview is progressing against your plan.

When you have the plan prepared, discuss it with the other interviewers so you all understand and agree what should happen.

Type it up and take a copy of the milestone plan to the interview. You have enough to do without trying to *remember* the plan.

Tip

Actors and actresses who achieve great stardom are so good that they seem to be natural. In reality, while they may be adorable, they are also perfectionists. They insist on take after take until every breath, every movement, every word is simply perfect. Now *you* are on the stage and should make your every performance perfect.

You shouldn't expect to make a perfect plan the first time, and neither should anyone else. I do expect you to revise the plan in light of your experience so it is near perfect after three or four interviews.

In the next section, you'll understand how the basis of selection has to comply with the law.

Keeping it legal

Local and national laws apply to employment and recruitment interviews. The laws prescribe what is allowed in an interview, and it is essential you understand what is and isn't legal.

For example, if you are interviewing several people in a day, it is often difficult to remember who said what. If you write "ginger hair" as a reminder on your paperwork, you are opening the door to a claim for discrimination.

Tip

Selecting someone through an interview is a form of discrimination. The reasons for your selection must be legitimate in every applicable case.

This isn't a reason to be over cautious. As I said earlier, preparation is the solid foundation which makes the manager, you, appear in control. Experienced managers have done this several times so will have the foundation. As a new manager, you can prepare and practice thoroughly and catch up on the experienced managers.

The anti-discrimination principles are simple enough even if the practice can be fuzzy around the edges. As a result, it's probably best if you simply avoid the edges.

Anti-discrimination laws vary from place to place, so you need to check the laws where you are. However, the basic principle is that you can discriminate for reasons relating to a candidate's ability to perform a task. You will measure this by asking questions and gauging the responses. What you must not do is assume a person's ability based on an observation or answer to a question about their life. You must not assume that just because I am 63 and overweight I don't have the ability to do a strenuous manual task. You must ask questions about my skill and performance of those tasks instead. To reveal my capability, ask about *performance*, not *characteristics* assumed to be linked to performance.

Search the Internet for "employment discrimination" to find more guidance about discrimination laws which apply to your location. Example sites are as follows:

> ➤ Cornell University Law School Legal Information Institute: `http://www.law.cornell.edu/wex/employment_discrimination`.

> ➤ U.S. Equal Employment Opportunity Commission: `http://www.eeoc.gov/`.

> ➤ UK Chartered Institute of Personnel and Development: `http://www.cipd.co.uk/hr-resources/employment-law-faqs/discrimination.aspx`.

> ➤ UK Government website—working, jobs and pensions section: `https://www.gov.uk/browse/working`.

To calm the candidate, you need to appear calm yourself. I spoke earlier about your performance being important. Remember, to the candidate, you are the organization, so you need to prepare yourself. The next section will help you do that.

Preparing yourself

Interviews are nerve-wracking, for both candidate and interviewer, until you are used to them. As a new manager, interviewing is something you don't have a lot of experience with yet. This may be your first conversation with your new team member, and you'll want to make a good first impression, so you need to prepare yourself enough to get out of the interview what you need to.

As a new manager, you need to develop the ability to perform at a moment's notice. You are in the spotlight. Perhaps you did some amateur dramatics? As kids, we all played make believe and adopted the stance and voice of our heroes and heroines. If that is what you have to do now, then find an appropriate role model and copy their behavior. You will develop your own style and your own brand in time.

You need to appear confident and not display symptoms of excessive nerves, which might include the following:

➤ A flushed face

➤ Trembling hands

➤ A nervous stutter

➤ Perspiring

➤ A faltering voice

When you practice your 2-3 minute introduction in front of people, make sure you also test your ability to control your nerves.

Practice your greetings in front of a mirror. Check for the following:

➤ A natural, welcoming smile

➤ Smiling eyes

➤ A steady gaze

➤ A sensible positive handshake: neither limp nor crushing

➤ A good form of words for the greeting: "Hello and welcome to..., my name is ..."

You should dress for the interview as you would dress for a meeting: relevant to your job, neither too smart nor too casual. First impressions endure, and you are a representative of your employer to the candidate. Dress and behave appropriately. Pay attention to the candidate; maintain eye contact and keep an open body posture, avoiding folded arms or legs. Switch off your cell phone and e-mail.

I have talked about the importance of performance quite a lot. The next section contains valuable tips on how to get into a high performance mindset when you need it, and conducting your first interview is exactly when you'll need it!

Preparing your opening speech

When you start the interview properly, to make sure your candidate feels at ease, prepare a 2-3 minute speech in the following format:

1. Welcome the candidate

2. Explain the purpose of the job

3. Describe how the vacancy came about

4. Tell them what your team is set up to do

5. Give some background about the organization

 Tip

In an interview, the candidate should be talking 80-90 percent of the time. So make sure you stick to 2-3 minutes!

Spend time writing out your speech (don't just do it in your head!) and practice it until you are word perfect. Practice saying it out loud; we speak faster in our heads.

Edit your speech mercilessly to give a taut, steady, but cheerful tone. I use the so what test. If it isn't immediately obvious what a word or phrase adds to the message, then edit it out. Aim to cut 20-30 percent of the words to leave plenty of space and a steady delivery. You don't want to rush the delivery.

Check the content of your speech with HR. You must avoid any declared bias that could be illegal. Your introductory speech could legally be part of the job offer. So, don't say my team will expand and everyone will get a promotion and a raise. Instead, say that you expect there may be promotion opportunities if things work out as you expect.

Test your speech on your friends and work colleagues. Ask them if it is accurate and has a friendly and welcoming tone.

You are now ready to begin understanding the structure of the interview.

Switching to performance mode

It would be wonderful, albeit boring, if life proceeded smoothly all the time. On the day of the interview, you intend to be well prepared, rested, up early, and in good form. What if you spill breakfast in your lap, jump a red light on the journey, and arrive late to find your manager waiting for you? A bad start to the day! All is not lost; you can learn to switch to "performance mode".

Have you observed how athletes take a minute to get into the zone before performing? Here is a mental trick I use when I have to perform and don't feel like it:

1. Sit quietly and remember how you felt when you were in top form, and practice recalling those feelings.

2. When you do, make a physical link to them.

3. Choose a physical link that is discreet so you can trigger it when you are not alone.

4. I make an O by digging my thumbnail into my right forefinger. Whatever your trigger, recall the feelings and jump into performance mode whenever you need it.

5. Practice it so you can jump at any time.

The next step is to prepare the candidate, to relax them so they are ready to be interviewed.

Prepare the candidate

All this preparation is irrelevant if you cannot communicate with the candidate due to their being on edge, nervous, and uncomfortable. This section will show you how to prepare the candidate.

Use your interview experience

You remember how it feels. You are brought into the room and sit in front of several stern interviewers. Your blood is pounding so hard in your ears you can barely hear what they are saying! It is a waste of everyone's time if you can't settle the candidate.

An interview is an exchange of information. You need to manage the candidate's (as well as the interviewers') nerves and composure for best communication to ensure you get the best out of them and have all the information you need to make the right decision at the end of the process.

This is the start of your management career, and your manager expects you to perform. Your ability to select the right employee(s) will carry your ambition forward and be reflected in your department's performance. This is why working through this book is so important. It is never too early to set yourself apart as different from the rest.

Believe it or not, you have an advantage as a new manager that other interviewers may not have—you have very recently been interviewed for a new position yourself! Use this experience to improve your own interview technique. Make a list of what was good and bad about your interviews as a candidate.

Think about the following points:

> ➤ Were you put at ease by the interviewer? Did the questions start before you had sat down? Did you feel so stressed you couldn't think or did the interviewer relax you?

> ➤ Was the interview process explained? Were you told how long the interview would be, what would happen during and after?

➤ Could you overhear the previous interview? Interviews should be private and neither overheard nor subjected to random conversation from nearby rooms or corridors.

➤ Did you feel you were rushed and unable to answer fully? There is nothing worse than feeling you weren't allowed to give the full answer; clearly "they" had already made up their mind! Much better to feel you had all the time you needed.

➤ Were you intimidated by the interviewers? You know the sort: weak managers who use their authority to bully. You won't allow this and will manage the interview responsibly.

➤ Was the room set up poorly? Inappropriate chair, lighting, line of sight obstacles? The interview room is no place for interrogation tricks but a space for as free an exchange of information as possible.

Use your own list of good and bad experiences and discuss them with HR to agree ways to improve the interview experience you're about to give to your candidates. For HR, this is just another interview in a long series of interviews. For you, this is an early opportunity to show who you are, and why you were given the manager's job.

To settle the candidate in the interview, you need to build rapport to put them at ease. The next section shows you how.

Building rapport

On first greeting the candidate, ask a few rapport building questions such as the following:

➤ Did you find us OK?

➤ Did you have a good journey?

➤ How was the traffic?

This normally takes a minute or two as the candidate is settling in the interview room.

Tip

If the candidate had a bad journey, do not ask if they will be able to get to work on time. This may be discriminatory.

Everyone tends to be nervous at first. The careful, thorough preparation you are doing will allow you to be confident, relaxed, and in control, so this conversation will be natural and welcoming. Be sure to make eye contact and use the normal nods and murmurs to demonstrate agreement in any normal conversation. Don't make the candidate feel you are just pretending to be interested in them. Use the conversation to relax them so they are able to answer the questions readily. Don't let the time run away though!

Make your own list of simple questions to build rapport and use them. You may find something in common with the candidate through their application: a college, children, or hobby perhaps.

We have now covered the basic preparation for interviewing. Before going on to the next chapter and learning some techniques of interviewing, please review the preparatory actions you need to complete in the following checklist.

Checklist

Before you proceed to the next chapter, ensure you have carried out all the tasks specified in this chapter. You need to be able to answer yes to the following:

➤ Have you discussed the job requirement with your manager to determine any change needed to the information?

➤ Have you collected the job advert, candidate pack, and interview questions from HR?

➤ Have you checked the job details and is the advertisement correct in every detail?

➤ Is the candidate pack correct?

➤ Have you agreed the interview structure and process with HR and the other interviewers?

➤ Have you decided how you want the interview room to be arranged?

➤ Have you worked through and measured or estimated how long each part of the interview should last?

➤ Have you prepared a plan with milestones to help you manage the interview?

➤ Have you written, learnt, and practiced the 2-3 minute introduction?

➤ Have you got HR's approval for the content of your 2-3 minute introduction?

➤ Do you understand how each interview question relates to a skill?

➤ Do you understand how the follow up questions are used to seek more detailed explanations?

➤ Do you understand your local Employment Discrimination laws?

➤ Do you have your own nerves under control?

➤ Have you decided how to dress for the interview?

➤ Have you developed a performance mode, a trigger, and practiced it?

➤ Have you identified the good and bad in your recent interview experiences?

➤ Have you discussed with HR how to use your recent interview experiences?

➤ Have you prepared and practiced your rapport building skills?

➤ Have you completed everything on this list?

Be sure you are competent in the first 19 points mentioned previously. Tick them off one after another as you achieve them. Before you tick number 20, ask yourself if you feel fully prepared to delve into the technique of interviewing.

Summary

This first chapter is about planning for an interview. By preparing thoroughly and carefully, you should be feeling confident about conducting your first interview. When you understand the process and know what is going to happen in the interview, you will feel more comfortable going into the situation, which will enable you to perform at the top of your game.

Together, we are building a tower of knowledge and experience of how to interview. This chapter is the foundation. If you do not build a solid foundation, the tower will always be rickety!

When you have completed each step in this chapter, you will be ready to learn about the interview itself. You will be well prepared, confident, and competent. You will be happy with the planned style and tone of the interview.

The next chapter explains interview techniques, neuro-linguistic programming, and body language. As an interviewer, you need to have an understanding of these to perceive the full range of communications in the interview process. A skilful candidate could use these techniques to mislead. I won't let that happen to you.

When you are ready, I'll be waiting for you in *Chapter 2, Starting the Interview – Greeting and Settling*.

Starting the Interview – Greeting and Settling

This chapter uses the preparatory work you did in the previous chapter as a foundation to develop your skills in managing the candidate and the interview process. These new skills include everything you need as a new manager to perform at your peak in the initial stages of the interview. You will learn how to practice these skills outside of the interview so that you give an outstanding performance in the interview.

In this chapter, you will learn to be completely comfortable with the following:

> ➤ Making introductions
> ➤ Observing the candidate

By the end of this chapter, you will have all the skills and knowledge you need to manage your first interview to the point of asking questions, which we will deal with in the next chapter.

I know you prepared your foundation skills in the previous chapter, but the skills you will develop in this chapter are slightly different. You will need to practice these new skills in real social interactions. There is no substitute for interacting with living, breathing people. You may find this difficult at first—embarrassing and at times even awkward. I will give you all you need to know to practice and become competent and confident even before managing your first interview.

You will finally polish your skills through the interviews you conduct. Interviews have their own peculiar stresses and emotions. But the more you practice these skills, even outside of the interview, the more experience you will have.

You have to work hard to become a good manager. Let's get to it!

Making introductions

Making an effective introduction is an essential part of the interview. It is crucial that you help the candidate relax and also relax yourself. You need to set the tone. If the interview begins well, everything that follows should be much easier.

Your first impression

You need to make a good impression on the candidate from your first meeting. It is very difficult to change someone's first impression of you. Therefore, it is important to represent you and your company as competent and capable throughout the interview process. As a manager new to interviewing, you have to walk a tightrope balanced between being neither under nor overconfident, neither too personal nor too formal.

Human beings make a quick "friend or foe" decision when they meet someone. This is prompted by the Four Tens, of which you need to be aware.

The Four Tens are as follows:

➤ The top ten inches of you

➤ The first ten steps you take toward the candidate

➤ The first ten words you speak

➤ The first ten seconds

The top ten inches include your grooming, hair, and smile—your facial appearance.

The ten steps toward the candidate relates to your smiling, your hand coming up to make a handshake, and making eye contact with smiling eyes.

This also includes your handshake and the casual talk as you lead the candidate to the interview.

This all takes place in the first ten seconds as you make your first impression.

We did preparatory work on this in the previous chapter, and now you have to bring it all together in the Four Tens.

Tip

Go to networking events to meet new people to practice the Four Tens.

Try to continue the small talk as you show the candidate to his or her seat. You then need to introduce the other people on the interviewing panel.

Introducing the panel

The introductory speech needs to be done succinctly. The point of the interview is to listen to the candidate, not you. Don't let the candidate, or another interviewer, start a long rambling conversation. If that happens, you will need to stop their conversation politely but firmly. We will work through how to do this in *Chapter 3, Conducting the Interview – Questioning and Scoring*.

You practiced the introductory speech in the previous chapter. Now you can deliver that easily and concentrate on the candidate.

Introducing the organization

Now is the time to deliver the explanation of the interview process you have prepared.

Tip

Don't forget to switch to performance mode if you need to.

Next, give your mini presentation on the organization, how the vacancy came about, and what the future may hold.

Ask the candidate if they have any questions about your explanations. As well as answering the questions, you should think about what the questions reveal, if anything, about the candidate's interest in the vacancy.

You will learn how to do this in the next section, and you'll discover why you have to be well versed in delivering those explanations.

Observing the candidate

As a new manager, you are likely to be more nervous than an experienced one. In the interview, you have to manage the process, keep to time, and so on. You need to deliver information in mini speeches. To observe the candidate, you need to learn about the following things:

> ➤ Misleading first impressions
> ➤ How eye movements indicate thinking style
> ➤ How body positions and movements can be read

You must be well versed in these tasks to leave you the thinking time to observe the candidate.

Tip

Think about learning to drive a car. In the beginning, there are so many things to remember to do. With practice, you learn how to drive without having to think about it.

First impression of the candidate

You are now seeing just how much is happening in the interview process. It is important that you continuously draw your thoughts together as you go through the interview to properly respond and direct your questions.

What is your first impression of the candidate?

> ➤ Does the candidate appear interested?

> ➤ Is the candidate alert?

> ➤ Is the candidate dressed appropriately?

> ➤ Will you work well with this person?

You should be observing the candidate's behavior from the moment you meet. Use the *Four Tens* prompts to think what is creating that initial impression. You know from your own experience as a candidate at interviews how to create a good first impression. Now you are the interviewer; how does the candidate present himself or herself? Have they made a special effort for you? Does the amount of effort taken equate to their interest in the job? Do you immediately feel inclined to trust this person to do their best for you? Be alert to these feelings and seek to understand their causation during the interview.

Bear in mind the job requirements. Not every job requires face-to-face interaction. If you are interviewing for a salesperson who visits potential clients, then the *Four Tens* are essential, whereas a friendly manner may be sufficient for a telesales person.

However, you need to be alert to bias here. Columbia University reports that one third more female musicians are appointed if the auditions are done from behind a screen so the panel cannot see the musician. Racial bias effects are greater and justified by doubts about qualifications and communication difficulty.

Be aware of your first impressions and potential bias. It is your job to find a good candidate, and bias reduces the available pool of talent and is usually illegal and irresponsible.

You may have heard interviewers say something like "I knew she was right for us the moment I saw her," or, "I could tell he was one of us instantly." That is because the interviewer was positively affected by the candidate's first impression. This is usually because the candidate is similar in some way to the interviewer. Equally, interviewers adopt negative first impressions when the candidate resembles someone they don't like.

Managers, experienced and inexperienced, make this mistake, but we can make sure you do not. You will be alert to the possibility and are going to choose the best candidate on the basis of their answers to the questions.

If you are aware of your own feelings toward the candidate, you can avoid this mistake. Now you have three things to do at once! You have to manage the interview, observe the candidate, and be aware of yourself too.

To enhance your skills, you are going to learn about two methods to structure your observations. The first is **neuro-linguistic programming (NLP)**, which has developed models (Bandler, Grinder, and others) of how a person's thinking style affects their eye movements.

Make a note

NLP is a model of how an individual's thinking style, physicality (how they use their body), and language are all inter-related. Each aspect can affect the others. You can talk yourself into a good frame of mind, think positively, and stand proud! For further reading, see the following books:

- *How to Influence Others at Work,* D. McCann, Heinemann Professional Publishing, 1988

- *The Structure of Magic,* Bandler, Richard, and Grinder, Science and Behavior Books, 1975

- *Syntactic Structures,* N. Chomsky, Mouton, 1957

Secondly, we explore the use of body mirroring as a communication channel.

NLP and eye cues

Eye cues need to be used with conversational clues to make a reliable judgment. Eye cues alone are not reliable evidence and, in any case, eye movement patterns can change with cultural differences.

Eye cues suggest preferred thinking and sensory styles. As an example, a person with a preferred visual style is less likely to be suitable for a telephone-based job. If you, as an interviewer, observe a sensory style that is inappropriate to the job, then you need to explore this in more detail. You will do this through the interview questions.

The eye cues that follow are for right-handed individuals. In your observations of the candidate, do you think they are right- or left-handed? Which hand do they use for writing or holding papers? Which is their active hand?

To understand why this can be important, we need to go back 2,000 years to the Latin language.

The Latin for left-handed is sinister, while for right-handed it is dexter. Approximately 10 percent of people are left-handed, and research suggests their brains are different and their manual skill is above the average. Yet, right-handed people are dexterous!

You will see in the eye cues why left-handed people were felt to be odd. Left-handers look left and right when right-handers look right and left.

The first two eye cues are looking up and to the left or right. A right-handed person looking up and to the right is probably imagining a scene, while looking up and left suggests a remembered scene. If you ask the candidate to describe a time they demonstrated a skill and they look up and to their right, this suggests they are imagining it not remembering it. How would you score a candidate who has to imagine the answer to your question? A left-handed person will usually send this misleading eye cue. They appear deceitful.

Don't make that mistake; be aware of the candidate's handedness:

The first eye cue suggests the person is making a picture in their mind and may be accompanied by a statement such as "I can see myself doing that". This form of imagery is a constructed image as opposed to a memory, and the person may appear in the image themselves.

If you have asked the candidate whether they can see themselves in the new job, this would be a good sign they are imagining the scene. It could also suggest a creative mind with an ability to construct pictures of how things could be done. In your questioning, you need to look for confirmation of what the eye cues are signaling:

This eye position suggests the person is recalling a real image. A typical comment would be "I see what you mean," or, "I see how that could work." A candidate showing this eye cue is likely to be telling the truth. You will need to make an assessment of the truthfulness from the words *alone first.* If you feel the words are false and contradict the eye cue it is possible the candidate is trying to mislead you. Not to worry, as only the most accomplished actor would be able to make a false impression through a complete interview. Careful observation will allow you to decide on a candidate's truthfulness.

Tip

Watch how actors use their eyes to suggest honesty, deceit, recall, and imagination.

"The eyes ahead defocused look" could be either type of visual sensory preference. You should be able to determine which one it is by listening carefully as described previously. Be careful when questioning people displaying this eye cue. They may not hear what you say! Let them come back to focusing on you before asking more questions. People who drift off into this inner contemplation for more than a second or two may not fit your skill specification. You wouldn't hire a cabdriver who had this tendency!

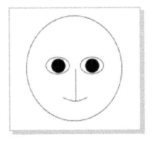

Make a note

I worked for a manager who did this. He only heard the first few words and then went inside to see what it meant. Until I understood this, I presented the situation outline first and then my solution, which he didn't hear. I learned to present my solution first and then the outline.

The next three eye positions all relate to a preference for audio communication. You must talk to this person to communicate instead of "showing" them a picture or letting them "feel" their way into a situation.

Typical responses would be "I hear what you say," or, "I like the sound of that." People with this preference are not so good with visual information, but they are good at conversations with customers and colleagues. They are likely to be very comfortable using the telephone. All abilities are relative of course. You will need to explore through questions, the range of ability across each sensory style that is relevant to the job:

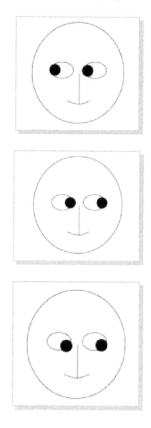

The last two eye cues indicate a physical, action-centered style. This style is about touch, physical feeling, and also emotion. Typically, this person will want, in fact need, to be in the center of the action dealing with physical things personally.

A person with this thinking style may say "I can grasp that idea," or, "That idea appeals to me."

You may want this person on the front desk dealing with people face to face and getting things moving. They would not be too comfortable on the telephone or dealing with visual data representations. Always use your questions to test the cues from the eyes. You would make a mistake if you put an action-centric person in a job requiring a lot of administration skills. If the eye cues suggest a tendency, then explore that fully with questions.

This style makes the person seem very confident, bold, and action-oriented. This may be the case, but check what the words say. Don't be overawed by these action power phrases! They are the easiest to learn! People who are confident and bold will have good answers to your questions that show their approach to life.

These eye cues may be fleeting, so you need to be very observant without staring and discomforting the candidate.

Don't forget to confirm your observation from the candidate's words. Don't be influenced by the words or the eye cues until you have decided they are honest.

 Tip
Start to observe eye and conversational cues in daily life. Practice makes perfect!

Some candidates may exhibit more than one style of eye cue. They may be a rare, well balanced individual able to choose the most appropriate sensory style, like an accomplished actor. Alternatively, they may be faking eye cues to distract you. You will usually be discomforted by this as the answers and the eye cues will be mismatched. People are very sensitive to eye cues.

If the candidate is able enough to fake the eye cues, you should be able to detect this using the next observation technique.

Body mirroring

The basic principle of body mirroring is that in conversation, people who like and agree with each other adopt broadly similar, but mirrored, body positions.

To an extent, body mirroring can steer a conversation, reinforce agreement, or display disagreement. You need to be aware of this non-verbal communication to assess and understand what is being communicated.

Tip

Watch how politicians and TV interviewers alter their body mirroring. Politicians are good at steering conversations to their own good!

This is a very effective way of communicating rapport, trust, and friendliness. As the interviewer responsible for judging the candidate, you have to be aware of this communication channel to be able to assess the content. You will then be in a position to weigh the non-verbal communication along with the candidate's answers. You can then decide if it all makes sense as a whole or if there are follow up questions needed to probe more specific abilities and characteristics. It is worth repeating that a candidate with good rapport building skills will tend to score higher in the interview. I want you to be aware of this possibility and to assess the answers to the interview questions without the bias that good rapport engenders. Equally, bad rapport has a negative influence of which you should be aware.

Body mirroring is a powerful non-verbal communication. For example, people in conversation will adopt a mirrored bend of the head: one to the left and one to the right. Another example would be how you rest your hands: clasped on the desk, one in your lap, or whatever. The actual position does not matter; it is the mirroring action that speaks volumes.

Tip

Make small adjustments to your pose and never mirror *exactly*.

Ask yourself if the candidate is actively managing the mirroring process. If you change your pose, does he or she quickly follow?

The candidate may become slightly uncomfortable during the interview. If so, what happens to the mirroring? A break in the mirroring signals disagreement. However, if the candidate is uncomfortable and mirrors the interviewer closely, that is unnatural. This would suggest the candidate is trying to manipulate the interview. As explained previously, people with good rapport building skills can get away with anything! President Clinton is a great example. He is revered by many despite his wayward behavior and impeachment over the Lewinsky affair.

However, you cannot take an observation of seemingly unnatural mirroring as proof of manipulation. Instead, this should alert the interviewers to this possibility and cause them to review their observations and assessment of the candidate's honesty. Ask yourself why the candidate is seemingly manipulating the panel. Is there something being hidden? Alternatively, is the candidate naturally open, friendly, and do they show interest in you? These are the building blocks of rapport. If the job you are filling needs these skills, you may just have found your ideal candidate!

Tip

I have sat on interview panels where the candidate's responses to the questions were seemingly irrelevant to some panel members. They had decided on the candidate in the first ten seconds and couldn't see past that bias.

Eye cues, body mirroring, appearance, and speech are what you must use to judge the candidate. You have to be aware of the non-verbal, as well as the verbal, communication to be able to weigh it all to be an effective judge.

Tip

Approach every interview with the expectation of an honest candidate. Be aware of the possibility of dishonesty and use your awareness of non-verbal communication to validate the answers to the questions. Remember, most people are honest.

Mistakes are possible though! Mostly, my managers recruited young people, and we had a well-proven interview, initial training, and probationary period before awarding a permanent contract (the local laws made this possible). A perfect new employee worked diligently until he was appointed to a permanent position. He immediately changed his behavior that day, complaining about instructions, refusing work, and seeking redress up the management hierarchy. We asked if he had a twin brother; the transformation was so complete. We then had to go through the disciplinary procedure to dismiss him.

You may make mistakes, but learn from them and remember that most people are honest. We have one final point to cover before moving on to the next chapter and the interview questions.

The candidate wants to make the best impression on you and be offered the job. Understand that this is a buying and selling process. You will need to have your eyes and ears wide open at the interview, absorbing every nuance of the candidate's words, body language, and behavior.

Thorough preparation is the only way to develop the competence that allows you to concentrate on the candidate rather than the interview process details.

To make sure you have completed every step, please work through the checklist in the following section. Identify anything you feel needs more work.

Checklist

We have worked through a lot of material in this chapter. You can overcome much of your inexperience by carefully understanding and practicing what you have learned. You will be able to gain experience using these skills outside of the interview room. This will leave you as fully prepared as we can make you with these skills.

You need to be able to answer "yes" to the following questions:

> ➤ Do you understand the *Four Tens?*
>
> ➤ Have you practiced the *Four Tens* in a social setting?
>
> ➤ Do you understand how eye cues imply thinking and sensory style preferences?
>
> ➤ Do you understand how the observed eye cues are supported by spoken words?
>
> ➤ Have you practiced determining people's sensory preferences in a real environment?
>
> ➤ Do you understand the principles of body mirroring?
>
> ➤ Have you used body mirroring in a real social setting to change the rapport between you and others?
>
> ➤ Have you practiced simultaneously observing and conversing with someone?
>
> ➤ Have you answered yes to every question on this checklist?

If you can, you should now feel that you can start an interview and settle the candidate with confidence.

Summary

I have shared critical skills in this chapter that will allow you to be fully aware of the informal and non-verbal communication in the interview room. You should be feeling much better equipped to properly conduct your first interviews.

I will repeat that you need to have practiced the skills in this chapter in any environment you are able to. You may find some of the techniques awkward at first, but it is better to get that behind you before the interview takes place.

You now understand how important it is to have learned and practiced these skills. In the interview, you are doing several things at once. As much as possible, everything you are doing should be automatic, almost unthinking, to allow you to observe the candidate.

We have covered a lot in this chapter, which together with the previous chapter will give you every opportunity to prepare for, and to be aware of, these important issues. If you thoroughly work through both chapters, you will have taken a big step toward gaining experience through practice. You will also be better prepared to learn quickly as you acquire more actual experience.

In *Chapter 3, Conducting the Interview – Questioning and Scoring*, you will learn and understand how the questions are used to get the candidate talking about their skills. The use of follow-up questions to clarify the ability and experience of the candidate is a key skill. We will work through several examples to make sure you can ask good follow up questions.

It is your job to ensure the candidate creates a factual impression. Much of this chapter has been about informal communication that gives rise to a subjective feeling that the candidate is right or not for the job. You need to understand what is creating this subjective feeling. When you understand the cause, you can test the feelings objectively through the primary and follow-up questions. In *Chapter 4, After the Interview – Agreeing and Deciding*, you learn about the consensus building skills you need to reach a common decision with your interview panel. The skills you learned in this chapter will avoid you having preferences that are not supported by your scoring of the candidate's answers. I want you to be confident in your final choice.

I know that if you have completed both checklists so far, then with the next chapter, you will be ready to manage your first interview. Together, we will make it a good one too!

Take a deep breath and move forward to the next chapter.

>3

Conducting the Interview – Questioning and Scoring

This chapter will show you how questions are used to assess and score the skills the candidate reveals in the interview.

You will need to have practiced all the skills we have worked through in the previous chapters to be able to make sense of the questions and answers, as well as to assess the candidate's score in the interview itself. In particular, you need to have practiced the NLP skills you learnt in the previous chapter. A good way of gaining confidence with NLP is to use these skills in your daily life; become familiar with these skills in a way that they become almost natural to you. This will ensure you are well prepared to observe the candidates' performances.

I need to show you the way questions can be used to clarify not only what skills each candidate has, but also what level of skill. To give you the greatest benefit, I will take you through an example of a job, its job description, skill requirements, interview questions, and scoring.

After we have worked through this, you will have learned how the interview works and you will have gained some interview experience from the example.

This chapter contains the following learning points:

➤ Hire for attitude, train for skills
➤ Active listening
➤ Avoid illegal notes
➤ Avoid thoughtless or unplanned remarks
➤ The Interview Simulator
➤ The closing question

Making a decision to hire someone is an important one. You and I have worked through a lot of preparatory material to bring you to this point. The attitude displayed by the candidate in the interview is an important factor.

Hire for attitude, train for skills

You may know this maxim. Changing a person's innate behavior is difficult, while training a new skill is relatively easy.

While a good attitude and high level of skill are not exclusive, you may not find that combination sitting in your interview room.

You will be making judgments on a candidate's aptitude and attitude from the moment you meet them. It is your job as the interviewer to match the candidate to the job. Their attitude will be an important part of that matching.

Remember that attitude is not visible to you except through the resulting behavior. Is the exhibited behavior suitable for the job? The candidate may display behavior suggesting an attitude towards risk based on a belief in luck. You might think carefully about employing a surgeon that behaves in this way! The attitude portrayed in the interview should be tested through questions. People can be nervous in interviews, so dig down in the questions to seek clear examples of relevant behavior.

A team of enthusiastic, high energy individuals would be great if only they knew what to do. How much you trade attitude for skill depends on who comes to interview and what you need for your team right now.

You may want to hire a mix of people, some very enthusiastic, some with a high level of skill. It all depends on the circumstances in your organization.

Think through who and what you want for your team. You may need people ready to change the world, but you probably need someone to do the routine work reliably and consistently as well. With a modicum of luck, you will find the ideal combination of candidates waiting to be interviewed.

Active listening

The first interview after lunch or the last of the day is not the easiest for the weary interviewer. Interviewing is extremely tiring because you are straining all your senses to build a coherent picture of the candidate. Active listening uses all the communication from eye cues, mirroring, the candidate's answers, and their application documentation to predict what they will say in response to your questions. Several hours interviewing is exhausting for anyone.

Active listening is not only essential if you are to get the most out of your candidates to reach an informed decision, but it is also an effective way to maintain your sharpness.

Tip
Practice active listening in your daily life to build your competence.

Listening can sometimes be a passive activity. You hear and try to make sense of what was said.

Active listening involves quickly thinking about what was just said and hypothesizing what the candidate will say next. The picture you are building of the candidate is the tool you use to predict what will be said next in response to the interview questions. When your predictions are largely accurate, so is your picture of the candidate. If your predictions are not accurate, then you will need to question around those contradictions and resolve them.

This interactive thinking will keep you awake and give you some assurance that you have judged the candidate well. You should keep these thoughts to yourself.

Avoid illegal notes

We covered this earlier in *Chapter 1, Before the Interview – Preparing and Practicing*, but it needs reinforcing now we are discussing the score sheets.

It may sound obvious, but do not make illegal notes about the candidate on the score sheet. Even something innocent, like a comment about the candidate's red hair to help you remember him or her, should be avoided.

Tip

If there is any doubt that a note may be discriminatory, do not make it.

A note about references or qualifications should be fine, however. The key thing is to think about the candidates in terms of their fit for the role; avoid any mention of their appearance and so on. When trying to remember them, your notes will ensure that you are focusing on the things that will ultimately help you to reach a good decision.

At the end of the interview, you should have an overall score for the candidate. We will cover how those scores are adjudicated in the next chapter.

Avoid thoughtless or unplanned remarks

The candidate may ask you what you thought of their interview. You should have planned an answer to this in the planning section of *Chapter 1, Before the Interview – Preparing and Practicing*.

Do not say you have or haven't got the job! That decision can only be made after seeing all the candidates and adjudicating the scores.

The candidate may ask about a specific skill and what more they can say to raise their score. You should answer honestly and give the candidate an opportunity to expand on their previous answer. Keep one eye on the clock though!

The Interview Simulator

The Interview Simulator that follows should give you an opportunity to see how all the different aspects of interviewing that we have been looking at fit together.

The job details are simplified and we will examine skills and questions so you understand how they are used in a real-life interview.

While of course the simulator can't prepare you fully, it should help you recognize an effective framework for an interview. When you are in an interview situation, hopefully you will recognize similarities to the example, which in turn should help you feel confident and give you direction when you may be feeling slightly uncomfortable.

First, you need to read through the setting of the job:

- ➤ Job details
- ➤ Job skills specification
- ➤ Interview questions
- ➤ Score sheet

Job details

The successful candidate will report to the manager (that's you!) of the newly formed **Vitamins Matter Too (VMT)** team which is part of a national organization.

The team is tasked with auditing the cafeterias in the organization's operating units to measure vitamin levels in the food and provide advice on menus and preparation.

It is expected that the VMT team will grow in number, and in two years or so will have the capacity to offer the service outside of the organization.

As the newly appointed manager, you have been asked to recruit an Office Manager whose job it will be to manage the Audit templates, the actual Audit documents, and organize a schedule between the operating divisions and the VMT staff.

This is a key role in the success of your VMT team. Your boss has stressed that she doesn't want to see you in your office all the time and expects you to be out in the field gaining experience, refining the VMT service, making a name for your team, and achieving her corporate objective of superior nutrition for the organization's employees.

You can see your VMT team is going to depend on the Office Manager, who will be the person organizing schedules and documents.

You will need to rely on the Office Manager to keep the operation running, and you may feel a concern that your reputation will be in their hands. Trust is essential, but these interpersonal issues rarely make it to the job description!

In reality, HR would prepare a full job description, job specification, and skills requirement. There would be a full set of questions with follow ups to assess the candidate.

The simulator uses a simplified skills specification.

The job skills specification

The following are the skills you are interviewing for in this interview simulation:

> ➤ Intermediate ability with Microsoft Word 2010 including the use of style templates and mail merge process proficiency

> ➤ Expert communicator and facilitator between organization, clients, and auditors

> ➤ Basic Microsoft Excel 2010 skills—can create client lists, worksheets, and schedules

You will be scoring the candidates on the basis of these specifications. The interview questions follow next to give you an idea of what to expect from your own HR department.

The interview questions

Each question relates to the same number job skill in the previous section. The follow-up questions to each question are sub-bulleted:

1. How familiar are you with Microsoft Word 2010, specifically style templates and mail merge? The following are the follow-up questions:

    > ➤ Can you tell me about a style template you created please?

    > ➤ How would you improve that template now?

    > ➤ How much have you used the mail merge function in Word?

    > ➤ What data sources have you used?

    > ➤ Which data source did you find the easiest, and which the most difficult?

2. How do you make sure your note taking and messages are accurate? The following are the follow-up questions:

    > ➤ What do you do if too many messages are coming in at once?

    > ➤ Do you know your limit and are you ready to ask for help when needed?

3. Have you any experience with using Microsoft Excel 2010? The following are the follow-up questions:

    > ➤ Have you used Excel to make a simple schedule?

    > ➤ Have you used Excel to make lists, of priorities for example?

Take some time to familiarize yourself with the skill specifications and their associated questions. Do you see how the follow-up questions ask for more specific detail allowing a better judgment to be made of the candidate's skill?

The candidate's answers provide the information for the interviewers to fill out the score sheet. You must do this in the interview. You can always review your scoring after the interview, but if you don't score each skill during the interview, you will forget pertinent information.

Instead of copying out all the information again, I can explain how the score sheet works using just one of the skills from the list.

The score sheet

The score sheet will have all the data such as the candidate's ID, the date, and the names of the interviewing panel. You have no need to think about that as your HR department will use a standard score sheet.

Typically, the sheet will show a skill, a space for your score, a factor, and the total for that skill.

Some of the skills in the job skills specification may be more important than others. To make the scoring easier for the interviewers, you are usually scoring on a scale of 0 to 10. If that particular skill has been given a weighting factor of 2 and you mark the candidate as a 7, then that will be worth 14 points in the final score.

You collected the score sheet from HR and all the factors have been agreed and settled. You can't concern yourself with the factors in the interview. Your job as the interviewer is to assess the skills on the basis of the candidate's answers to the questions.

Now I'm going to show you how to do that. I'm going to take you from a skill for the job, through the questions and answers, and show you how to judge the score for that skill:

> **Skill**: Reasonable ability with Word 2010 including the use of style templates

>> **The opening question**: How familiar are you with Microsoft Word 2010 and style templates?

>> **The candidate answers**: "Yes, thoroughly conversant, I use it all the time."

That is a claim that you now need to test with the follow-up questions. Now you ask the question: Can you tell me about a style template you created please?

Tip

Don't forget to use eye cues to inform your judgment

Observe the candidate closely. Are they remembering or inventing? Are they still relaxed and body mirroring? Do they take a long time to answer or is the answer immediate?

The candidate answers slightly awkwardly: "I made a style template for the kids' swimming club I help organize."

You may now judge that "thoroughly conversant" was overstating the skill in the candidate's first answer. You need to decide if the candidate was just nervous or was trying to mislead you. You may also think that some volunteering role experience of a Word style template is still valid experience.

To answer that question—is the candidate's experience sufficient—ask the next question: How would you improve that template now?

The candidate could answer that no improvement is possible or a particular modification would be helpful. You need to judge what the answer means.

Given the previous answers, how would you score "no improvement possible"? Either the template is perfect or the candidate lacks experience to see the improvement possibilities. Are you doubtful that the template is perfect? This would suggest that the candidate is not that experienced with style templates but has at least produced one example for the kids' swimming club.

The candidate has shown a basic ability to create Word style templates. You know what your VMT team are tasked to do. There are document styles to create but not that many. The styles need to be correct to give the right image and you will be approving them anyway. How would you score this candidate? Would you score them a 6, 7, or 8?

Tip

Judging candidates' scores is relative. If you score the first candidate as all 0s or 10s, you have left yourself no room to go lower or higher with the next candidate.

Given the advice in the tip, let's discount the 8, leaving us with 6 or 7.

What do you feel about the candidate's "thoroughly conversant" answer? If it was nerves, I'd propose a score of 7, but if it was an attempt to mislead, then perhaps 6 is more appropriate, or even 5 if you feel that strongly about it.

You can imagine a number of different candidate answers. Work through what you would look for to support or discount those answers. You can use the dialogue we have just worked through to give you more ideas.

Not all the answers will be quite as convoluted! Now for a straightforward example:

➤ **Skill**: Ability to mail merge documents in Word 2010

> ➢ **The opening question**: Have you ever used the mail merge function in Word 2010?

> ➢ **The candidate answers quickly**: "Yes, to produce letters and catalogs."

This may be another attempt to overstate the candidate's skill. How does this answer compare to the "thoroughly conversant" answer? "Yes" is much more direct. Now you need to do all the observations on eyes and mirroring and move on to the next question: What data sources have you used?

The candidate answers straight back: "Access and Outlook."

Does this feel like an honest answer? The response was quick. You need to test a little more to make the judgment. You ask: Which data source did you find easier, and which one more difficult?

The candidate answers immediately: "Outlook and Access are fine. I haven't used Excel much and find that difficult sometimes."

Do you think this is an honest, balanced answer? It is possible that admitting a weakness in Excel is a smokescreen to hide a complete lack of experience in mail merge! Is the candidate keeping eye contact with the interviewer during this answer? Are they fidgeting or looking uncomfortable and untrustworthy?

The candidate's answers have been delivered quickly and with a seemingly balanced view. This would suggest the candidate is being truthful, as only the most accomplished fraudster can maintain a false impression in an interview. How would you judge this?

Would a score for this skill as a 7 or 8 make sense? This leaves room for a better score if a subsequent candidate has all the abilities the questions seek.

There is an art in crafting interview questions which your HR team will have prepared for this interview. The interviewer has a responsibility to get the "most accurate answer" from the candidate. Sometimes, that takes some perseverance:

➤ **Skill**: Expert communicator and facilitator between organization, clients, and auditors

>   ➢ **The opening question**: How do you make sure your note taking and messages are accurate?

>   ➢ **The candidate answers straight back**: "I focus on one thing at a time."

Is this a sensible answer do you think? So far so good I think, but we would want to dig deeper. You ask: What do you do if too many messages are coming in at once?

The candidate replies with some uncertainty: "I would make a list and say I'd call back in a little while."

That sounds like a reasonable answer. How do you feel about the candidate's ability to work accurately under pressure? Are you convinced? Are the candidate's answers or style affecting your decision?

You ask the next question: Do you know your limit and are you ready to ask for help when needed?

The candidate answers quickly and with a hint of pride: "Yes, the service call administration is quite busy, but we do get unpredictable surges in demand. If there has been a TV program about the dangers of letting the servicing slip we get a storm of requests. When I see the requests running at a high level for half an hour, I call for help."

This is a positive answer, and it feels like the candidate is being truthful, don't you think? This answer is from the candidate's current job behavior and should be a good predictor of how he or she will behave for you. Would you score this highly, 7, 8, or 9?

This final example shows the interviewers struggling to reach a scoring decision:

> ➤ **Skill**: An ability to create simple lists and schedules in Excel 2010
>
> > ➢ **The opening question**: Have you any experience of using Microsoft Excel 2010?
> >
> > ➢ **The candidate answers slowly, saying**: "I keep a tally of expenses for the service people but I have not used Excel much really."

Your VMT team needs to be scheduled by the Office Manager, and an Excel spreadsheet seems the obvious way. This lack of Excel experience in the candidate is a little worrying. You ask the direct question: Have you used Excel to make a simple schedule?

The candidate responds quickly with a "No", probably showing some signs of embarrassment that they can't match that need.

Do you think you could easily train this candidate to create and run schedules on Excel? You have a good feel by now of the candidate's abilities with Access, Outlook, and Excel. You need to make a judgment on how to score this person.

You ask one last question: Have you used Excel to make lists, of priorities for example?

The candidate answers: "Yes, as I said, for expenses. I also made a list of tasks for my manager to prioritize last month."

It seems clear that this candidate has little experience of Excel, although they could probably be trained fairly easily. How would you score this skill? The skill that is being tested is specific, and the answer was "no". Perhaps a score between 3 and a generous 5 is appropriate?

Tip

Think about the questions and answers in this simulation to decide how you judge the scores and why. The interviewers usually broadly agree on the score.

The interview process is about hearing evidence from the candidate, testing it with follow up questions, and then judging the result.

The simulation we have just worked through is just like a real interview. The only difference is you aren't trying to observe the candidate's behavior and manage the interview to schedule at the same time!

Pause to reflect for a moment—you just worked through your first job as an interviewer. Your head may be spinning at the moment from your thoughts about the process. The interview simulation is worth re-reading several times. You will find new questions, new angles to explore each time. The more you think and judge, the more experience of interviewing you will take to your first real one.

If I have done my job well you should be feeling much more confident now. Just like a flight simulator, you have experienced and learned some key things about interviewing. They don't let you fly solo at first and you won't be interviewing alone either for the first time.

Make a note

I suggest you close the book and go and get a drink of something. Your head needs time to digest all that information.

We still have a few things to cover in regard to good interviewing practice.

The closing question

It is always a good practice to ask the candidate at the end of the interview if they have any questions. A candidate who has researched your organization and thought about the job and what further opportunities this may bring will likely have questions burning inside them! An insightful question from the candidate indicates they have given thought to how the job may suit them.

This is your final opportunity to observe the candidate:

> ➤ Do they show enthusiasm?

> ➤ Are they excited at the opportunity or faintly bored?

> ➤ How do you rate their questions?

Some candidates may find the interview very tiring and will just want to get away as quickly as possible. A candidate who is still showing the right attitude and is fired up, eager to know more, and shows signs of wanting to work with you will stand out from the crowd.

Make a note

When I was a candidate, I always asked if the interviewers had all the information about me they needed, if they were unhappy with any of my skills, and then asked for the job! If you get asked that, refer to the scores and be honest about the weaker skill judgments.

Answer the questions as best you can but without making any comment whatsoever regarding their likelihood of getting a job offer. You cannot know this until all candidates have been interviewed, the scores have been computed, and the panel has adjudicated the scores.

Candidates often ask "what happens next", and this will be the standard process you apply in your organization that HR will usually manage.

After answering any questions, thank the candidate and have them escorted back to reception. You can now make sure your score sheet is complete, move around, and get a drink for yourself. You deserve it!

We have covered a lot in this chapter, and you hopefully feel like you have had a simulated interview experience.

There remains the checklist and summary to complete this chapter.

Checklist

This chapter builds on the foundation work in *Chapter 1, Before the Interview – Preparing and Practicing*, and the structure in *Chapter 2, Starting the Interview – Greeting and Settling*, and has brought these elements all together in the form of the Interview Simulation.

By now, you should be able to say yes to all these points before we move on to the final chapter:

> ➤ Have you decided on the best mix of attitude and skills from the candidates interviewed?

> ➤ Have you practiced active listening?

> ➤ Have you fixed firmly in your head what you can't write or say in an interview?

> ➤ Do you understand how the job skills specification is based on the job description?

> ➤ Do you understand how the interview questions are derived from the job skills specification?

> ➤ Do you understand how the score sheet is based on the interview questions?

> ➤ Have you worked through each example question and answer in the Interview Simulator and considered how you would score the candidate?

> ➤ Do you understand how the follow up questions are used to clarify the level of the candidate's skills or your understanding of their ability?

Of course, conducting an interview is not as simple as following a formula every time, but with an understanding of what to look for and what questions to ask, you should be more comfortable dealing with the nuances and details of any interview.

Summary

This chapter's Interview Simulator has given you the closest experience to a real-life interview that I can create in a book.

We have worked through how the job skills required ultimately connect to the interview questions and the scoring.

We have examined examples of questions and answers, including follow up questions and answers, with a variety of score judgments.

Good interviewing is about being a good judge. It is also true that good managing is about good judgment. I know you appreciate how important this first managerial task is because you have read this book and made it to here!

You may have felt some pressure in the simulation from having to observe and think simultaneously. A real interview is demanding for the interviewer. Your preparation, practice, and simulator experience will increase your ability markedly.

You should now feel you have a lot of experience in the key elements of interviewing.

When you are looking to hire, HR will do much of the preparatory work, as we covered in *Chapter 1, Before the Interview – Preparing and Practicing*. HR or you may decide who to invite for an interview based on their applications. You will have their applications prior to the interview and you should familiarize yourself with them. This will lead you to focus your questions on relevant issues and is part of normal interview preparation.

You should be careful not to prejudge a candidate as first impressions, even those gained through a document, can be misleading and difficult to change.

We have one last point to cover in the next chapter. Interviewers may form different opinions of candidates. There is a process of adjudication and joint decision making that comes after the interview to ensure that you select the best candidate.

We will work through the decision making process next.

4

After the Interview – Agreeing and Deciding

In the final chapter of this book, I'm going to show you how to reach that all important hiring decision. You have your score sheets from the interviews filled out with individual skill scores, which are factored according to the importance of that skill, and you have a total score for each candidate. The scores will be used to rank the candidates; the highest score will be ranked first, then second, and so on. It is not likely that you will find a candidate with the maximum score.

Do you think it likely that each interviewer recorded the same score for each candidate?

Life isn't like that, unfortunately. You need to discuss, agree on a common score, and then make a joint decision.

I'll share some tips from my experience that will make this process easier.

In this chapter, you will learn:

> ➤ How to review your own candidates' skill scores
> ➤ How to set minimum acceptable skill scores
> ➤ How to reach an agreement on the candidates' ranking
> ➤ How to make a shortlist
> ➤ How to get supporting evidence of the candidates' claims
> ➤ How to manage, decide, and make special adjustments to scores

After the steady build up in the previous chapters to the summit of the Interview Simulatitor, you can think of this chapter as a plateau; an opportunity to consolidate everything and learn how to pick the best candidates. The experience and learning you received from previous chapters are important, but the really valuable output of the interview is your decision. Luckily for you, the evaluation process outlined in this chapter is done post-interview and is far less stressful.

You will need to understand your own and the other interviewers' observations, but you haven't got the stress of running the interview to schedule, observing the candidates posturing cues, and questioning.

Remember, making the right hiring decision is vitally important to your career. Your first hire will carry your approval and be an example of your vision for your team. The performance of your team is your responsibility and is a measure of your performance as a manager. A good leader builds a great team. Now we need to make sure the information you have gathered throughout the interview process is used to hire the right person for the job.

Review your candidate scores

Inexperienced interviewers have trouble with the calibration of their scoring. It is important you remember that you are making a comparative judgment, not an absolute one. The score sheet you are using will usually weight some skills more heavily than others: they are more important to the job performance. It is perfectly acceptable to choose a high scoring candidate overall who has a low scoring relatively minor skill.

You may remember in the Interview Simulator that I recommended mid-range scores particularly for the first candidate. You needed to avoid scoring a 10 when the next candidate might be even better! You need substantially justified reasons to score in the extremes. This will come with experience of interviewing. You just have to leave yourself some room to score above or below.

In this section, you will learn how to:

> ➤ Tap into your intuition regarding the scores

> ➤ Understand why your intuition is grumbling

> ➤ Review your scores

> ➤ Take your grumbling intuition and share it

Throughout this learning journey, we have discovered facts, observed other people, judged them, and come to a score. Now we have to weigh your intuitive insight.

Intuition says the scores are wrong

Hopefully you have had a good night's sleep between the final interview and your discussion about which candidates to place on the shortlist.

You have your scores nicely tabulated, but you don't like the resulting ranking. Something doesn't quite look right.

Instinct, intuition, or gut feelings are not to be ignored. If nothing else, you need to be confident the scores are correct. You don't want to hire someone and always be waiting for the dreaded day when they prove your negative feelings were correct. You want to be positive about the decision you make.

You will need to think about the individual candidates' skill scores and confirm they are your best judgment. Do this for each candidate and for each skill. There is a process for amending your scores, and this follows when you understand why your intuition is unsettled.

Understand your intuition

You may feel you have been more or less generous in the score you have awarded a candidate. This is *not the time* to adjust the scores to get the result you want. Be fair with any adjustments to the scores. If you find yourself adjusting an individual score by more than plus or minus one, you are probably *not* being fair.

Do not adjust the scores to achieve the candidate ranking you feel is right. Review each of the skill scores fairly, using the same measure. A score must mean the same for every candidate; a score of 7 is the same across all the candidates.

Unfortunately, it is often the case that despite the *small* adjustments you made to the individual scores, your intuition leads you to still have doubts about the ranking of some candidates.

Tip

Learn to recognize the signs that your intuition is communicating concern. Physical effects include sleep disturbance, stomach pains, a feeling of unease, and straightforward discomfort.

Think about the candidate that seems to have the wrong ranking. This could be affecting three candidates or more, the troublesome ranked candidate and the immediate neighbors.

Is there anything that stands out as different between these candidates that may not have been captured in the interview process? What is your intuition restless about? You will know when you have resolved the aberration—your intuition will respond by relaxing the physical effects you feel.

Review your scores

Let's work through an example. You have two candidates with total scores just one point apart. The higher scoring candidate has a lot of experience in one of the skills needed and is extremely confident, so confident in fact that the candidate actually said they know all there is to know about the subject! The lower scoring candidate had some relevant experience and scored very highly, but admitted they could always learn more and be better.

If your intuition is grumbling, there were probably other different instances of "I know it all" in the interview that may have led to good scores.

An interview is a snapshot taken in time. The job the successful candidate will do will go on week after week, month after month, and will develop in ways not entirely predictable. Is your intuition telling you to score the candidate who is more willing to learn more highly?

Tip

Find a quiet place to think and uncover what your intuition is telling you.

Did you find the reason behind each ranking "error" you are concerned about?

I would expect you to find the reason most of the time. Make a note of your doubts and the reasons for them ready for the next stage.

Setting minimum acceptable skill scores

The job specification identifies a number of skills and will usually weigh some more heavily to emphasize their importance. You must consider if there are minimum skill levels that are essential to the job.

It may be the job is just like many others in your organization, in which case the minimum acceptable skills are likely to have been determined by HR. You should have the opportunity to vary this if you can supply the missing skill in some other way. Perhaps you can restructure the process, deliver some training, or spread the workload over more than one person to give coverage of all the skills.

Be careful with the team-based approach as you don't want to find the only person with a key skill is demanding recompense for their rare skill. It is a matter of degree. Make sure you have a very good reason, such as an outstanding candidate, which you want to include in your team-based approach to get all the skills you need.

Tip

A business I was working for was rapidly developing its product technology, and to keep pace with the technical demands, I specified a degree-level technical qualification for new recruits. These new employees were some 40 years younger than some of the team who had been doing the job for years, but they were fearful of the new technology's demands. The new graduate staff went through our six month product training program with flying colors. When it came to working with the product and resolving problems, they were completely lost. They did not have the ability to conduct thought experiments and hypothesize what could be wrong. Their problem solving consisted of random acts in the hope of striking it lucky! I specified a training course, to be delivered by our local technical college, to raise their ability to hypothesize experiments and determine results. The existing staff's problem solving skills had been deeply undervalued so was not weighted heavily on the score sheets.

Technology is a leading cause of process change, with a consequent change in the skills needed. You cannot recruit someone to a job "for all time". If you think you can see 5 years into the future and predict what your team will be doing, you are mistaken. Adaptability is an important skill for you and your team. This is why attitude can be more important than aptitude, albeit with a minimum skill capability.

You now have to reach an agreement with the rest of the interview panel.

Reaching a consensus with the panel

Despite everything, interviewing is a subjective, judgmental process. It is unlikely that all the interviewers rank the candidates in exactly the same order.

Sometimes, an interviewer will observe or miss something, and their score is markedly different from the rest of the interview panel.

In this section, you will learn how to do the following:

> ➤ Deal with your unresolved intuition issues
>
> ➤ Identify and resolve ranking differences between the interviewers
>
> ➤ Decide on a consensus ranking of the candidates

The inexperienced manager needs to be well prepared to present his or her nagging doubts and defend the candidate scores. At the same time, you need to be open-minded and to engage with the rest of the panel's opinions to move toward a consensus. This can be a difficult balance for the inexperienced manager. However, if you make sure that you have thoroughly prepared by thinking through your scores and doubts, then you will impress the rest of the interview panel.

You can use your NLP skills to read your interview panel's non-verbal communication. If you are all sitting nodding in agreement with mirrored body language, you will know you have an agreement. If someone is sat with arms crossed in front of them as a defense, they are indicating they are not open to be dissuaded from their view. Are their eye cues suggesting they are remembering or imagining the candidate's skills? You will need to explore the reasons why they hold this opinion so strongly.

Remember the open and closed question choices. To uncover reasons, you need open questions, and to test for agreement, you need a closed question.

Your ability to manage the interview panel's consensus building will increase your credibility with your peers.

When your boss quietly asks them how you performed, they will be likely to respond very positively: "amazingly well!"

Sharing your intuition's doubts

If, despite your efforts to understand your doubts, you still have unresolved ranking issues of your own, you now need to share them with the interview panel.

This is *not* the case that you are simply inexperienced at interviewing. In my experience, 10 to 20% of candidate scores just don't feel right.

Ideally, the panel will all share their doubts on their rankings. They probably have some of the same doubts as you.

To give an example, consider a candidate who said they have the experience you are seeking but subsequent answers did not satisfactorily show the individual's contribution to the team's performance. You are left with a nagging doubt that the candidate was part of the team and not a leading contributor. You may have written "contribution?" on the score sheet, and despite the follow up questions, you may not have had this concern completely relieved.

Talk them through your concerns and make use of their perspectives to help you to resolve your doubts. You can use your new NLP skills to better understand your co-interviewer's points. Don't forget though that there is always a limit on time—as well as patience—in a meeting.

Resolving ranking differences

The first step is to compare your candidate ranking with the other interviewers. Write up a list in rank order for each interviewer. Are there any major discrepancies? You all need to understand why this candidate has received such a widely varied score. Did one interviewer spot something? Or did they perhaps miss something? Discuss it and find out what caused the score variation.

Tip

At a company I used to work for, the Board were looking for a Chief Executive and had developed a comprehensive job specification around our vision for a product. The tight specification left us with two candidates to interview, although one was clearly ahead on paper. Each candidate received a full day's interview including meetings with stakeholders, desk exercises, and addressing a meeting. Both candidates performed well. The interview panel sat to consider whom to hire. I was concerned; my intuition was kicking that the leading candidate before and during the interview appeared to hold some views contrary to our vision. We carefully revaluated the candidate's answers and found evidence of the contrary views. We dug deep into the scores and could see that the answers to questions around our vision were not particularly strong. The candidate had put on a strong, confident performance, and we had been swayed by the strong character. Much to everyone's surprise, we offered the job to the other candidate. If you can all see that one of the skill scores is out of line between you, then consider adjusting it in light of the information that was observed or missed.

This is an iterative process. Keep doing it until the candidate rankings are *broadly* similar.

Sometimes, your intuition will still be signaling dissatisfaction. By now, I would expect the interview panel to be largely in agreement, so you are probably not alone in being perturbed.

As an example, consider that despite all the previous work, you feel that Candidate C is better than Candidate A. You all feel the skill scores for both candidates are sensible but the ranking is wrong. Now it is time to review the weighting factors that multiply the individual scores.

You can see in the following score sheets that while the scores are close, Candidate A is ranked ahead, scoring 60 points compared to 58 for Candidate C.

Skills 1 and 2 are weighted with a factor of 2. This doubles the score for these two skills as they are considered very important to the ability to succeed in the job.

After a discussion with the interview panel, you might consider that skill 1 is even more important and should receive a 3 weighting.

Adjusting the weighting factor for skill 1 alters the candidates' scores as follows:

Score Sheet Candidate A				Score Sheet Candidate C			
	Score	Factor	Weighted score		Score	Factor	Weighted score
Skill 1	6	~~2~~ 4	~~12~~ 24	Skill 1	8	~~2~~ 4	~~16~~ 32
Skill 2	8	2	16	Skill 2	8	2	16
Skill 3	8	1	8	Skill 3	6	1	6
Skill 4	8	1	8	Skill 4	5	1	5
Skill 5	8	1	8	Skill 5	7	1	7
Skill 6	8	1	8	Skill 6	8	1	8
		TOTAL	~~60~~ 72			TOTAL	~~58~~ 74

You will need a good reason to change the weighting factor by 100 percent. This is not an exercise to adjust all the weighting factors to make your favorite candidate rank first.

It may be that you are stronger or weaker in one of the skills yourself, which could be a reason for altering the skill weighting factor for your first employee.

Ensure that the interview panel unanimously agrees and make a meeting note as to why the weighting factor was changed.

Do not adjust several skill factors to achieve the ranking result you "want". If you have to defend your collective decision to alter the factors, it has to be on the basis of clear, sensible, and recorded reasons.

Tip

I once needed to replace a Purchasing Manager to operate in a software-based **materials requisitioning planning** (**MRP**) environment, sourcing and negotiating as required. There was an urgent need to reduce capital held in inventory and purchase prices. There were many well qualified people interviewed as business conditions were tough and businesses were failing. The job specification called for strong MRP, sourcing, and negotiation skills. To test their negotiation ability, the final question was "when did you last get a discount?" With one exception, the candidates had to think hard to find an example. The exception just laughed and replied "I always get a discount". She had been a PA to a creative design house outsourcing their designs for manufacture. Her MRP experience was none, her sourcing experience was very limited, but negotiating was in her DNA. My experience included MRP and international sourcing, so I put together a training program to impart that knowledge. I changed the skill weighting so negotiation was much more important than the others. Interestingly, this ranked all the candidates in a more acceptable fashion. She was stunningly successful and is now a qualified Purchasing Manager. A problem can occur if a candidate is very strong in those secondary "would like" skills but weak on the main skill.

I do caution against expecting the ideal candidate who scores 10 out of 10 in every skill. You will be extremely fortunate to have such a candidate. You need to select a competent candidate.

However, it is perfectly sensible to set a bar for particular skills, and even total scores, so that those falling below the bar can be eliminated from consideration.

This is a useful technique if you have interviewed a lot of candidates and need to reduce the amount of data you are attempting to consolidate.

Once again, the important and correct method is to discuss it and make a meeting note about why and where the bar was set.

Reaching a consensus

When you broadly agree on the rankings, draw up a table on a flip chart or screen so you can all see how the rankings vary.

This figure shows you how to do that:

Ranking Table

	Interviewer 1	Interviewer 2	You	Combined Rank	Overall Rank
Candidate A	1	2	2	5	2
Candidate B	6	6	5	17	6
Candidate C	2	1	1	4	1
Candidate D	3	3	4	10	3
Candidate E	5	4	3	12	4
Candidate F	4	5	6	15	5

Put up the ranking by each interviewer of each candidate.

Candidate A was ranked first by Interviewer 1 and second by Interviewer 2 and you.

Add the rankings together—*1 +2 +2*—to give a combined rank.

Mark the lowest rank total as overall rank 1, then the second lowest as 2, and so on.

You now have a combined rank of the candidates as follows:

1. Candidate C.
2. Candidate A.
3. Candidate D.
4. Candidate E.
5. Candidate F.
6. Candidate B.

Are you and your interview panel all happy that this ranking is sensible?

If you are all happy with no sign of opposition from your intuition, then you have succeeded in ranking the candidates.

Making the shortlist

You can use the candidate ranking, shown in the previous section, for this section:

1. Candidate C.
2. Candidate A.
3. Candidate D.
4. Candidate E.
5. Candidate F.
6. Candidate B.

You can now apply the bar you have agreed on, judging Candidates E, F, and B to be below the needed standard.

Tip

Don't be afraid to find that none of the candidates are suitable. You may need to adjust the operating processes, refine the score sheets, and re-review the candidates.

You now have your shortlisted candidates:

1. Candidate C.
2. Candidate A.
3. Candidate D.

Supporting evidence

HR will now take the shortlist and start the job offer procedure.

Many organizations have been lax in the past in checking on previous employment references and claimed qualifications.

I'm sure your organization isn't one of those, but just be sure the evidence is checked.

Special adjustments

You may have altered the weightings on a particular skill in the knowledge you could compensate for that by making an adjustment elsewhere in the operating process.

Perhaps the candidate has some special need that has to be catered for in your work environment.

You need to have the plans ready to make the adjustments when the candidate accepts the job. You don't want your new employee discovering on their first day that you have "forgotten" to do what you promised.

Please work through the checklist and revisit any points you need.

Checklist

By now, you should be able to do the following things:

> Understand your intuition regarding the scores

> Know the process to review your scores

> Manage your intuition's issues to resolve them

> Resolve ranking differences between the interviewers

> Produce a consensus ranking of the candidates

> Discuss and agree minimum skill scores

> Prepare the shortlist

> Specify the evidence needed of previous employment and qualifications

> Plan the adjustments needed to operations to suit your new hire

Summary

In this chapter, you have learned how to work with your intuition to uncover your doubts about candidates' skills, your scoring, and the weighting factors.

Judging skills on the basis of answers to questions is a comparative process. The inexperienced manager needs to plan the scoring of the candidates to ensure that too high or too low scores given to the initial candidates does not restrict the range of scores for the subsequent candidates.

You can see how the others on the interview panel may face the same doubts from their intuitions. You can practice listening to your intuition before the interviews in everyday social interactions.

Finally, you learned how to shortlist the candidates ready for HR to make job offers.

The pre-employment checks on job references and qualifications are usually part of HR's normal process. Please make sure that is the case!

You have learned the need to plan the "special adjustments" you promised in the interview. You don't want to forget to do that.

Good luck!

Inevitably, in a book telling you how to interview, I have included a lot of difficulties, problems, and the occasional catastrophe! Now is the time to reassure you that it isn't always as difficult. This example shows how you can be fortunate. My Operations Managers were asking for a resource to provide quick specialist tools, fixtures, and facilities. These required a mixture of mechanical and electrical engineering skills and an ability to listen to the Ops Manager's people and deliver something quickly, experimenting if necessary. The **Financial Director (FD)** would not agree to a permanent contract, so I wanted someone past retirement age (no longer legal), so there was no problem terminating the contract. I also didn't want to pay too much so the person had to live nearby to avoid traveling costs. I advertised in the local newspaper and had one application from someone who lived a mile distant. He had worked maintaining the land-based connections of undersea cables on islands strung across the Pacific Ocean. He was a self starter and could do anything! He was also retired and a very intelligent, softly spoken man. He was extremely successful and played a big part in raising the performance levels. When we couldn't afford him anymore, he offered to work for nothing as he enjoyed it so much!

Despite all the difficulties you may face finding the ideal candidate, sometimes you will be lucky. You always have an ability to vary the skill specification to make your own luck. But be careful not to move too far from the established specification until, and unless, you are confident you understand, and can cope with, the ramifications.

Together, we have worked through, and you have practiced, the basic skills, the observational skills, the interview questioning skills, and the post-interview selection process.

When you have completed all the activities in this book, you will be ready to interview.

More than that, your interview panel colleagues and candidates will be impressed, and you will be prepared and confident every time you enter the interview room throughout your career.

I wish you every success in your management career.

www.ingramcontent.com/pod-product-compliance
Lightning Source LLC
LaVergne TN
LVHW081348050326
832903LV00024B/1363